THE
TREEHOUSE
BOOK

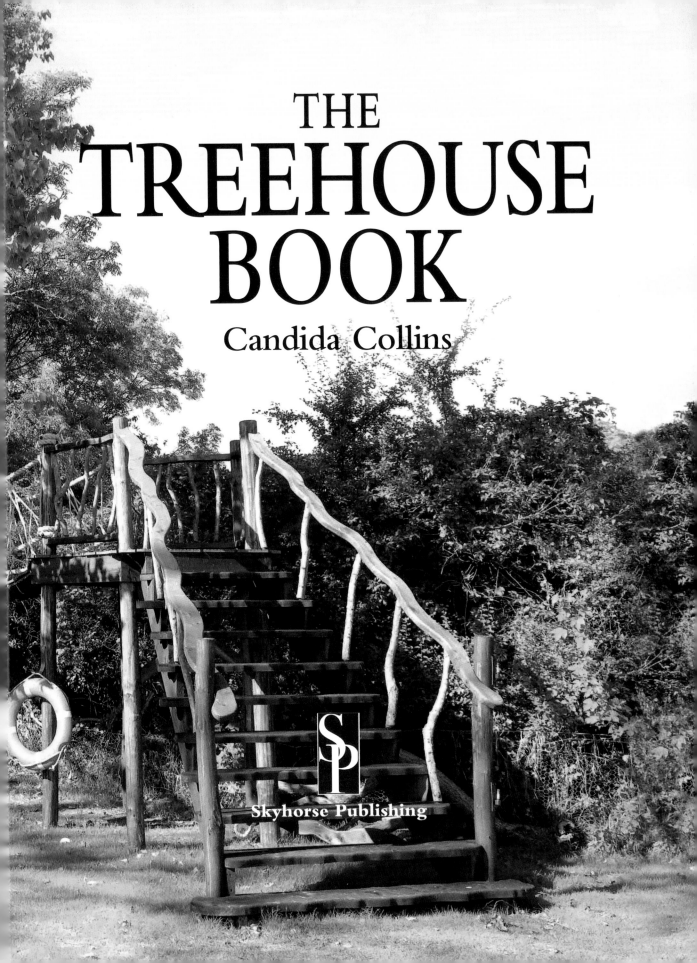

THE
TREEHOUSE
BOOK

Candida Collins

Skyhorse Publishing

Skyhorse Publishing books may be purchased in bulk at special discounts for sales promotion, corporate gifts, fund-raising, or educational purposes. Special editions can also be created to specifications. For details, contact the Special Sales Department, Skyhorse Publishing, 555 Eighth Avenue, Suite 903, New York, NY 10018 or info@skyhorsepublishing.com.

www.skyhorsepublishing.com

10 9 8 7 6 5 4 3 2 1

Library of Congress Cataloging-in-Publication Data

Collins, Candida.
  The treehouse book / Candida Collins.
     p. cm.
  ISBN 978-1-60239-761-3 (hardcover : alk. paper)
  1. Tree houses--Pictorial works. I. Title.
  TH4885.C65 2009
  728'.9--dc22

                              2009022669

Designed by Sue Rose
Printed in India

Acknowlegements

Pages 12 to 160: Images © Blue Forest (UK) Ltd

Blue Forest (UK) Ltd
1 Bensfield Farm Cottages
Wadhurst
East Sussex
TN5 6JR
UK

Website: www.blueforest.com
Email: info@blueforest.com
Tel: +44 (0) 845 5190 599
Tel: +44 (0) 189 2750 090

Contents

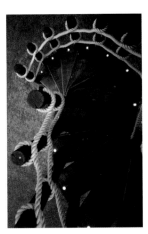

The History of the Treehouse

Safe from predators and other marauding tribes, the treehouse was one of the earliest forms of human protection. The safety of the treetops was especially popular in the tropical forests of the Pacific region and Southeast Asia. The occupants of these houses in the sky came and went via large wicker baskets, hauled up and down by their fellow tribesmen. They brought up their provisions in the same way. Once native peoples found how convenient a treetop life could be, they continued to live that way for centuries. Even today, this arboreal protection is still valuable to many tribal peoples. The ground level environment in densely forested areas is not at all conducive to a comfortable life. Hoards of wild animals, impenetrable vegetation, and the lack of light combine to make life very difficult. When he discovered Tasmania, Captain Cook wrote about how the indigenous people coped with their forest environment by living high in the treetops, in "hovels built of sticks and covered with bark." The Tasmanian tribesmen used fire to hollow out huge forest trees to make them more suitable for their treehouses.

There are still many good reasons to prefer a high life in the trees. The Kombai and Korowai tribes of Papua New Guinea live in treehouses built a hundred and thirty feet above the ground to avoid the unfriendly advances of the neighboring Citaks, a tribe of active head-hunters.

Rather than being "tree forts," most contemporary treehouses are built for purely recreational purposes. Most are constructed from environmentally low-impact and beautiful natural materials that may also include reclaimed and recycled elements. They appeal to our modern desire for eco-friendly, organic buildings that don't make an impact on their surroundings. In particular, building a treehouse does not require any ground clearance or the destruction of woods or forest. Since the 1990s, treehouses have become increasingly popular, and specialist tree building companies now offer a huge range of lavish and imaginative structures. These can be treated as extensions to the home rather than a makeshift play space for kids. By making a trip to the garden so much more inviting, treehouses fit into the modern concept of the garden as an extension to our living space, an "outdoor room" for relaxation and play. One of the added benefits of building a treehouse is that they are often

Alnwick Castle treehouse.

FACING PAGE, TOP LEFT **Julia Hill**

FACING PAGE, TOP RIGHT **Raised patio on the treehouse—an escape from mundane, everyday life.**

FACING PAGE, BELOW **A leafy home for treehouse dining.**

ABOVE **Pitchford Hall Treehouse**

exempt from building-control regulations.

As well as being a symbol of play and fun, the modern treehouse has also become a symbol of protest against the misuse of the environment, especially road building and tree felling. Julia Butterfly Hill is particularly well-known for her 738-day treetop vigil to save a California Redwood. For over two years, she lived on two small treehouse platforms built two hundred feet above the ground to protect a group of giant trees from being felled. In 2003, members of the environmental organization, Greenpeace, lived in a treehouse for over five months to save the forest trees of Tasmania's Styx Valley.

Historically, the treehouse soon became less of a primeval necessity and more of a charming part of civilized life. Writing in his famous book, *Naturalis Historica*, the Roman philosopher Pliny the Elder (23 to 79 A.D.) described how the extravagant Emperor Caligula "held a banquet in a tree...in a dining room large enough to hold fifteen guests and the necessary servants." The treehouse was built into a huge plane tree at his estate at Velitrae, and his leafy dining experience included entertainment by acrobats and jugglers. Although Pliny believed that Caligula was insane, the idea for treetop dining spread.

In the more ascetic Middle Ages, Franciscan monks used modest "tree rooms" for meditation. Hindu monks still use similar structures to free their contemplations from earthly considerations.

In complete contrast, the flamboyant Medici family built several treehouses during the period of their oligarchy in Renaissance Italy. Cosimo Medici, the Grand Duke of Tuscany, constructed an extraordinarily elaborate treehouse, complete with its own water supply and a series of fountains. His son Francesco built the even more bizarre "Fountain of Oak" treehouse. Twenty-five feet above the ground, the structure was reached by two massive spiral staircases. It was fitted with a huge marble dining table and had its own spectacular water feature. The treehouse subsequently became the must-have accessory for every Florentine garden.

One of the first royal personages to climb

ABOVE **Treesort treehouse.**

into a treehouse was Queen Elizabeth I. She is reputed to have dined sumptuously in a treehouse built in the boughs of a massive linden tree. In 1832, the young Queen Victoria continued this royal tradition when she visited the famous Pitchford treehouse, from where she watched the local hunt. Pitchford is now one of the oldest treehouses in existence. It was built as a miniature version of Pitchford Hall, which Victoria accurately described as "striped black and white (and built) in the shape of a cottage." Known as "the tree with a house in it," the Pitchford treehouse is now open to the public.

In the nineteenth century, the Romantic poets used simple treehouses as an escape from mundane, everyday life. With their poetic yearning for the beauty of nature—and their fascination with everything remote and mystical—the treehouse was an ideal platform from which they could view the world below and free their imaginations.

At almost the same time, the French took their passion for fine dining into the treetops. Entrepreneur Joseph Guesquin created a two-hundred-table restaurant, high in the branches of a row of enormous chestnut trees. The meals were hauled up to the diners in baskets. He located his unique dining experience in the town of Plessy, which he re-named Plessy-Robinson in the 1870s. This was a double tribute to the *Swiss Family Robinson* and *Robinson Crusoe*. As the town is just west of Paris, the restaurant was soon attracting society diners, including Balzac. They were charmed with the beauty of eating among the leaves and squirrels and the rambling roses that grew through the trees.

More conventionally, Winston Churchill built a treehouse for his children at his beloved country estate Chartwell Manor. Located in Kent, England, Chartwell is now owned by Britain's National Trust and can be visited by the public.

Treehouses have also been the subject of many literary tributes. Perhaps the most famous is Johann David Wyss's *Swiss Family Robinson*, where a shipwrecked family build themselves a treehouse. In Tolkein's *Lord of the Rings*, the Galadhrim, or elfish "tree people," live in treetop telain or flets (wooden platforms built in the branches), while *The Simpsons* have their Treehouse of Horror. Perhaps it is the literary popularity of treehouses that has embedded the concept so deeply into our collective consciousness.

In modern times, treehouse resorts have become popular around the world. Perhaps one of the best-known "Treesorts" is in Takilma, Oregon, where a cluster of sophisticated treetop dwellings hosts the World Treehouse Association conference, designed to celebrate "life on a limb."

The most lavish treehouse ever built dates from the twenty-first century. The Duchess of Northumberland commissioned a $4.4 million treehouse complex at her home, Alnwick Castle, in northern England. Supported by 16 mature lime trees, 10,000 nails and 280 tons of timber were used in its construction. The complex consists of several turreted cottages and a 120-seat restaurant. It is the size of two Olympic swimming pools.

Although twenty-first century treehouses may be equipped with LED lights, double glazing, broadband, bathrooms, and game consoles, they retain the feeling of being an escape hatch to a simpler life. They are still places to think, play, read, hide, dine, rest, entertain, or just enjoy the view.

Blue Forest   www.blueforest.com

Blue Forest is a family-owned company that offers a complete range of bespoke treehouses, from fantasy dens for children to sophisticated entertaining spaces for adults. Andy Payne started Blue Forest in 2003, and the company has now built a reputation for their highly imaginative designs, their consummate craftsmanship, and their active concern for the environment. The company prides itself on using only sustainably sourced timber and materials that do not damage the host tree. Blue Forest is also passionately concerned with forest conservation and preserving wildlife. Andy and his brother Simon (who is also part of the Blue Forest team) grew up in East Africa where they were able to enjoy the beauty and adventure of the great outdoors. This love of nature has been instilled into the Blue Forest ethos, which is to promote adventurous outdoor living and bring people closer to the natural world—to transport their clients to a treetop world above the stresses of everyday life. The team has now completed a wide variety of treehouse projects around the world, from Central America to the Borneo rainforest.

Blue Forest designed and built all of the treehouses featured in this book. Their work epitomizes the variety and sophistication of today's treetop living.

Castle in the Trees

This fantastic treehouse was built on the beautiful grounds of one of Ireland's most magnificent and historic country houses. Finished with cedar lining and shingles, the style of the treehouse windows closely reflect the Tudor Gothic architecture of the main house, which dates back to the seventeenth century. It is supported partly by the huge boughs of a stupendous and ancient oriental plane tree and partly by a series of sturdy wooden pillars. The treehouse has a magnificent octagonal tower and a wooden balcony for taking in the lovely views. It features beautiful stained-glass windows, including one in the art nouveau style that represents romantic red roses. A curving wooden staircase, complete with a rope handrail, approaches the treehouse. The interior of the house is also lined in cedar and includes a built-in window seat.

The most eye-catching feature of the Castle in the Trees is its two-story octagonal turret. This upscale treehouse took three months to build.

The treehouse windows give a new perspective on your garden.

A wraparound timber balcony gives the most wonderful views across the statuary-strewn gardens and lake of this historic home.

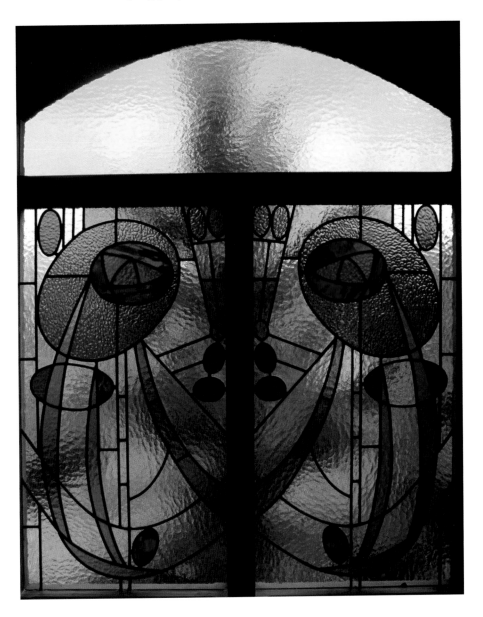

Living the High Life

This upscale treehouse project is designed for luxurious family living. It features two separate lofty retreats, one for the children and one for their parents. The complex features a dramatic canopy walkway, an adventure play area and an assault course. The design brief was to provide an aerial complex for family enjoyment and an unusual venue for entertaining friends. The adult treehouse has beautiful conical thatched roofs, and its walls are clad in hand-split oak shingles and cedar tongue-and-groove boards. The interior features a kitchen, bathroom, and a large living area for treetop dinner parties. The children's treehouse consists of three medieval towers connected by rope bridges. A secret trapdoor leads into a game room, complete with plasma television and game console. An eighty-yard zip wire delivers the children to an exciting assault course.

RIGHT **The round, fairytale towers of the children's treehouse has a witch's hat roof, covered in cedar shingles. The arboreal setting is truly magical.**

The treehouse has a great calming, positive effect

An unusual venue for entertaining friends...

LEFT **The fully-equipped kitchen even has its own wine coolers. Its walls are clad in mellow cedar tongue-and-groove boards.**

ABOVE **The vaulted ceiling inside the conical roof is beautiful. The low-level lighting complements the natural light from the small windows and makes the cedar glow.**

BELOW **The trapdoor leads into a secret game room, equipped with a large plasma screen television and game console. The room has beautiful views across the garden.**

Armonia Naturale

Commissioned by a nature-loving Italian family in the vicinity of beautiful Lake Garda, this stunning treehouse is the perfect country retreat. The structure has been specially designed to blend into the stunning alpine scenery that surrounds the crystal clear waters of the lake. The treehouse looks out into the evergreen tree canopy, and the balcony at the front gives the family an ideal vantage point from which to enjoy the local flora and fauna. The treehouse has some special features for the family to enjoy, including an ingenious little birdhouse with a discreet peephole positioned on the inside of the treehouse so that the family can watch the baby birds hatching. The treehouse itself looks like a little birdhouse perched in the branches. It is constructed from indigenous pine planks and cedar wood shingles.

The back of the treehouse is covered in cedar shingles. Inside, the building is clad in pine boards.

The treehouse is equipped with a practical bathroom.

The lower image shows the ingenious peephole into the birdhouse.

High-Tech Hideaway

This mind-blowing treehouse was built in response to the client's brief to create a James Bond–style hideaway for his children. It is located on a beautiful private estate in Athens, Greece. The treehouse is the epitome of luxury and has been designed to accommodate some fantastic high-tech gadgetry. This includes a state-of-the-art biometric security system, featuring fingerprint locks and a CCTV system. This controls five ultra sharp, color night vision cameras, which are positioned to cover an entrance or exit to the treehouse. The control center allows the user to move and zoom the cameras and take still shots or video footage of any intruders. The interior of the treehouse is equipped with every comfort including a kitchenette, bathroom, and an entertainment area equipped with a plasma screen television, game consoles, and digital photo frames.

High-tech on the inside, the treehouse is constructed from completely natural materials: wood and thatch.

The treehouse sits in the pine treetops

The main door to the treehouse features biometric security. As every secret agent knows, security is vital!

House for the Fairies

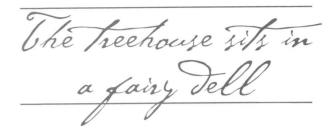

The treehouse sits in a fairy dell

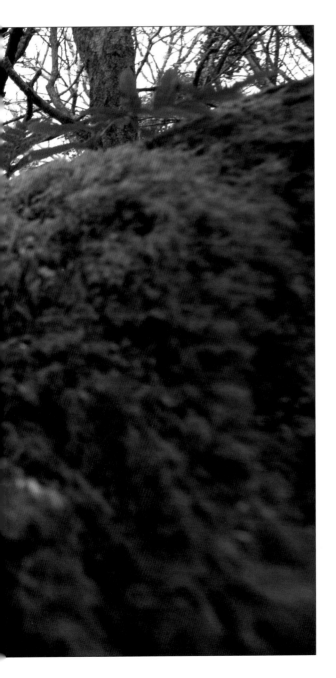

The lucky owner of this treehouse has created a fairy den in the beautiful oak woodland adjoining her house. Positioned deep among the trees, the treehouse sits on a wooden frame, rather than being supported by the oaks themselves. It is built from cedar planks and shingles and has a steep-gabled, shingle roof. Nothing is square or straight about the Fairy House. It has no right-angled corners, and even the glazing bars are delightfully wavy. Not only do the fairy-loving client and her family enjoy using this treetop retreat, but a little door has been specially constructed to also let in any passing little folk. A small woodstove heats the fairy house with logs from the surrounding woodland, so that it is comfortable year-round.

The secret Fairy House sits deep in the beautiful oak woodland next to the client's home.

The cozy interior must feel warm and welcoming to any passing little folk.

◆ **the treehouse book** ◆

Ramshackle Den

A wonderful focus for safe adventures

This is a very traditional treehouse specially
designed to be an exciting den for children.
The client's desire was to provide a safe and
adventurous place for his children to play in
the family's wooded garden. The finish of the
structure is deliberately rustic and rough
hewn. It sits in a marvelous setting, deep in
mature woodland of mixed native trees,
including beeches and silver birches. The
trees form a protective circle around the den.
The treehouse is built on an exciting play
platform that is constructed onto a robust
wooden framework. This also supports a

slide, climbing wall, and swings, and leads
onto a wonderful aerial bridge. This walkway
leads to this magical playhouse in the trees
and to a second adventure deck. Constructed
from timber planks and woven ropes, it
meanders high up in the treetops, through
the leafy branches. A neat feature is the
basket and pulley that brings up secret
provisions to the den for adventurous
picnics.

The treehouse platform is also equipped with a climbing wall, slide, and swings.

High in the branches, the aerial rope bridge leads to a second adventure deck.

The rustic treehouse
hides in the
branches

Treetopia

Treetopia is built in the shade of a magnificent cedar, constructed on a wooden platform.

Built in the shade of a stupendous and ancient cedar, Treetopia actually sits on a wooden platform, which is approached by a winding wooden staircase. Built in a charming hexagonal shape, the playhouse is also a more traditional treehouse, specially built for the enjoyment of children. The treehouse is constructed in half-log lap style and roofed in traditional cedar shingles, which will mellow down into a silvery gray. The inside is clad in sweet-smelling pine planks. Its hexagonal shape is echoed in the window cut into the front door. The structure provides a safe and adventurous place for children to play in the beautiful woods and plays host to a number of play accessories, including a climbing wall, rope-bridge, slide, and swings. A second adventure deck is also included in the package, while a rope-operated winch winds up a basket of supplies to the "Treetopian" world.

The treehouse plays host to a number of play accessories, including a climbing wall.

Cliffside Lodge

This beautiful and luxurious treehouse and lodge complex is set in a magical private garden. It reflects the style and character of the main house, which dates from 1886, having beautiful thatched roofs, handmade doors, and leaded windows. The treehouse and lodge nestle in the huge boughs of several massive trees, clinging to the rocky

The beautiful treehouse and
lodge are both thatched

slopes of a river gorge. Access to the
treehouse is via a dramatic rope bridge built
from the second floor veranda of the main
house, which then crosses the river to the
smaller lodge. The interiors of two treehouse
buildings are lined with western red cedar
and lit with low profile, recessed halogen
lighting. They are furnished with beautiful
nineteenth-century antiques, paintings,
ornaments, and books. Balconies, which give
spectacular views across the river, surround
both the treehouse and the smaller lodge.

This rope bridge leads back to the main house and onwards to the lodge.

A Room with a View

This complex has a perfect combination of features to accommodate both the adult clients and their children. The treehouse and drinks deck have been built to make the most of the stunning views from this house and garden. The children's treehouse is equipped with a traditional swing, rope ladder, fireman's pole, and zip wire. It is built in a traditional log cabin style and roofed with cedar shingles. It has pretty, mullioned windows and is lined with pine planks. The hexagonal drinks deck is supported by a wooden framework, fastened around the trunk of a massive pine. It is a blissful place to relax while the children play.

The treehouse is attached to the drinks deck via a rope bridge. The treehouse has its own lookout balcony.

A Fairytale Castle

The treehouse is set inside a secret garden

Deer, grouse, and pheasants can be seen wandering nearby

The luxury treehouse features an eighteen-foot-tall tower with an eye-catching solid oak, gothic arched window. A spiral staircase winds up inside the structure to a viewing platform.

Tarifa Eco Lodge

This upscale treehouse consists of a collection of three eco-lodges located in the hills of Andalucia on the Spanish Costa de la Luz. Each lodge enjoys incredible views of Africa across the Strait of Gibraltar. The lodges are highly insulated to withstand the harsh environment. The buildings are equipped with the latest in solar energy and water-heating solutions. They also have composting toilets and a water catchment and purification system.

The lodges are built into the hillside, among the low trees of this semi-arid landscape. They are constructed from oak planks and built on wooden platforms. The roofs are covered in cedar shingles. The extensive balconies that wrap around the lodges offer the guests the chance to enjoy the stunning outlook in supreme comfort. Inside, the oak-lined lodges are extremely inviting, simply furnished, and completely practical, with fully equipped kitchens and glowing log stoves.

Stunning views across the Straits to Africa

What could be more
enjoyable than a
barbecue with this
mesmerizing view?

The lodges nestle into the
landscape

The lodges have been built to leave
the lightest possible footprint on
the wild landscape. Their wooden
structures melt into the hillside.

Amberley Castle

The magnificent ramparts of Amberley Castle are nine hundred years old. They tower sixty feet above the beautiful gardens beneath.

This treehouse was created on the grounds of Britain's only medieval castle hotel, Amberley Castle. Hauntingly beautiful, it has been hidden away for over nine hundred years. Both King Charles II and Queen Elizabeth I have slept within the sixty-foot-high walls of this imposing fortress. The design brief was to create a beautiful and luxurious treehouse that reflected the romantic ambience and stunning architecture of the hotel. It also needed to be suitable for year-round use, and capable of hosting business meetings, weddings, and private parties.

The exterior of the finished treehouse features solid oak, gothic arched windows and doors, hand-split oak shingles, and cedar planks. The roof is thatched with traditional water reeds. The interior is lined with western red cedar and features low profile recessed halogen lighting and a beautiful oak floor. Access is via an elegant spiral staircase.

Lakeside Paradise

A lakeside paradise on a private island

This lovely, sylvan treehouse is set in a perfect location: a private island on Italy's Lake Garda. The client asked for a comfortable focal point to his island hideaway, somewhere that would be both a great place to read and relax and a venue for barbecue parties and entertaining. The extensive veranda built at the front of the treehouse provides ample space for this. The exterior of the treehouse is finished in softwood tongue and groove cladding, and it is roofed in cedar shingles. The many windows make the most of the sunlight and dappled shade, and there is a special sunbathing deck. Although this aerial complex is built in and around the trees, no fixings have been driven into the living wood so that the trees can thrive and grow normally.

A world of sunlight and dappled shade

This aerial complex features a covered veranda and walkways, almost hidden in the tree branches. It has wonderful views of the waters of Lake Garda.

The Enchanted Forest

This wonderful forest haunt looks like a hybrid of a fairytale castle and witch's house. It makes the most of its stunning riverside setting and the mature trees that also support the rambling structure. The treehouse is set in mature woodland, which consists of mixed native trees. The two-story complex is built on a series of decks and bridges, including a lower one, which jetties out over the river. This would make a wonderful place to fish from. A wide swinging seat hangs from chains attached to the top deck.

Inside, there is a large playroom and adjoining turret. A ladder leads up through a secret trap door into an upstairs hideaway. This fantastic den is fully equipped with a log-burning stove, hammocks, lighting, and power. The treehouse is also equipped with a rope-driven pulley to lift up supplies.

A hybrid fairytale castle and witch's house

Oak Tree Den

This wonderful den sits high in the leafy treetops, almost invisible to outsiders. The massive boughs of an ancient oak tree support the structure, which also has a second adventure deck. The design brief was to provide the client's children with a safe and adventurous place to play. The treehouse is built to look as rustic as possible. It is constructed from softwood planking and cedar shingles, and the veranda fence is made from natural tree branches. In keeping with the "play" theme, the den is equipped with a number of accessories, including a climbing wall, rope bridge, slide, and swings.

The den sits high in the leafy treetops

Woodland Haven

This extraordinarily quirky treehouse was designed as a secret hideaway for the children. The main structure stands approximately two-and-a-half yards above ground level and, despite appearance, is primarily supported by solid timber posts. The exterior of the cabin is finished in a deliberately eccentric combination of rustic tongue and groove claddings and randomly fixed cedar shingles (which are also used on the roof). This all helps to make the structure fade into its woodland setting. A separate treetop deck is hidden away in the woods and is linked to the main structure by a long rope bridge. The treehouse is also equipped with a slide and climbing wall.

Although the treehouse is built around a massive old tree, the structure is supported mainly by a series of solid timber posts.

With its eccentric fenestration and intentionally random cladding, the treehouse looks like a Hobbit hole.

A rope bridge links the main treehouse to a separate treetop deck that has been deliberately hidden in the woods.

Tanglewood Treehouse

Tanglewood Treehouse was built to provide a safe and adventurous place for the client's children to use while exploring their fantastic garden. It has been built to be suitable for year-round use and is equipped with a television for wet-weather entertainment. The extensive aerial complex also includes several secondary treetop decks and "crow's nest" lookout, which are linked to the main structure by an exciting and extensive network of rope bridges and ladders. A good range of play equipment is also included in the set-up, including a zip line, swing, and slide. The main treehouse is equipped with an extensive veranda from where less adventurous grown-ups can enjoy wonderful views of the sun-dappled garden. This space has been provided with suitably rustic wooden chairs. Inside, the treehouse is furnished with child-sized playroom equipment.

An extensive network of rope bridges links the main treehouse with satellite decks and treetop lookout.

*A treetop playroom
in the branches*

A place to enjoy the sun-dappled garden

The main treehouse has a wonderful veranda on which the grown-ups can settle to watch the fun. The rustic furniture has been specially made for the setting.

A Room in the Branches

Although it is small, this pretty little treehouse is perfectly formed. It has an idyllic lakeside setting. From the back, the treehouse looks like a well-fenestrated birdhouse, set high in the trees, but the front of the structure is equipped with an extensive deck. This means that, while this treetop den can provide a solitary hideaway for reading and relaxing, it can also be used for casual entertaining. The treehouse is constructed around a massive tree, and a collar-shaped wooden framework supports it from below.

A birdhouse set high in the treetops

A wooden walkway leads from the treehouse and opens
out into a sizeable entertaining platform that is
supported by the boughs of a nearby tree.

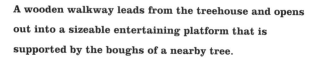

it has an idyllic lakeside setting

Treetop Dining

This stunning, oak-framed treehouse is built high in the boughs of a massive, three-hundred-year-old oak tree. It was built in the gardens of an oak-beamed country house, and the design brief specified that the timber matched that of the house. It is roofed with some nicely-weathered cedar shingles. The idea behind this fantastic open-air platform was to provide a wonderful and unusual space for outdoor dining and a focus for outside entertaining. The oval treehouse is fifteen feet long and is reached by a sweeping spiral staircase. At night, when the deck is illuminated, it looks like a large lantern hanging in the tree and gives wonderful views across the manicured garden. The platform is equipped with a bespoke oak dining table that seats up to twelve people and a selection of comfortable chairs. A pulley brings up the supplies.

A mid-air dining room
suspended in the trees

Inspirational Home Office

This truly inspirational home office makes the most of its owner's stunning country garden. There is a short "commute" from the main house across a twenty-five-yard rope bridge before you arrive at the treehouse office. This is sheltered by a grove of substantial oak trees. The office is designed to have every comfort and convenience and be a practical workspace. It is equipped with heating, lighting, power, broadband, and a telephone line. The treehouse is constructed around the bole of a beautiful tree and is partially supported with sturdy posts. Inside the treehouse, a bespoke desk has also been fitted around the living tree trunk. The light-filled room is both inviting and cozy, with comfortable chairs to sink into and enjoy the tranquil views. The high conical roof, windows, and folding glass doors make the space airy and open to the garden.

This twenty-five-yard rope bridge is one of the most enjoyable commutes imaginable. It leads to a veranda outside the office.

Badger's Den

Badger's Den is a traditional children's treehouse, constructed in the style of a rustic log cabin. It is surrounded by an attractive grove of sycamore trees and screened by woven willow panels. The hexagonal structure has a shallow roof covered in cedar shingles. The interior of the small cabin is paneled with cream-painted planks and is complete with a built-in secret cupboard, beamed ceiling, lighting, and pretty gingham curtains at the four-paned windows. It is furnished with child-sized play furniture and cozy cushions. The Badger's Den treehouse is built on a wooden platform supported by substantial wooden posts that is also equipped with a long slide and a winch to haul up supplies. A wide veranda offers views back across the garden. A long, attractively woven rope bridge approaches the den, high above the garden.

Badger's Den is a lovely, warm, and cozy den for year-round play. Its welcoming furnishings provide a charming refuge.

Outside, the veranda acts as a convenient adventure platform. It is equipped with a long slide and winch.

Treetops

This picturesque treehouse is set in wild and beautiful countryside. Treetops is so extraordinary that the Discovery Channel featured it in its Tree Team series. The main structure of the treehouse has been built approximately twelve feet off the ground, around the huge trunk of an ancient pine tree. The structure is cleverly built around several large boughs that seem to sprout from its walls. The exterior of the house is finished with a combination of rustic, waney-edged sawn timber cladding and cedar shingles, that are set in a random pattern. The inside of the treehouse is lined with softwood tongue and groove cladding. A second drinks deck for the adults has been built high up in a neighboring pine tree, situated on the edge of a rocky outcrop. This secondary structure offers wonderful views across a fast-flowing river.

Treetops is set high in the pine branches. It is attached to its massive tree with a substantial wooden collar.

The treehouse has wonderful views across the wild countryside

Leafy Retreat

The design brief behind this beautiful treehouse was to create a place with multiple possibilities; a great place for the kids to play, a wonderful entertaining space, and a hideaway from the world. The finished structure includes a series of arched windows and glazed double doors, a natural cedar shingle roof, and a rustic timber exterior. On the inside, the treehouse is fully lined with cedar and a polished floor. It also features an extensive range of home comforts. These include under-floor heating, lighting, a fireplace, and a flat screen television. The beautifully furnished treehouse also has a cozy window seat from which to enjoy the stunning views. It is constructed on a substantial platform that is approached by a winding staircase. Although this retreat is not actually built into a tree, it blends into the attractive woodland setting.

This Leafy Retreat is set into a luxuriant woodland setting, with panoramic views across the beautiful garden.

Building a Treehouse

**Depending on the scale of your vision, and the extent of your budget,
you can construct a homemade treehouse from simple building supplies;
or, you could decide to commission something a little more ambitious.**

Perhaps the most important thing to consider when planning any size of treehouse is its location. Is there a suitable tree where it could be situated? Can the structure be either fully or partially supported by the tree or will an additional framework be needed? Perhaps more importantly still, how will the finished treehouse relate to its surroundings and what added dimension will it offer to the enjoyment of the site? Will it offer fabulous views? Will it be a great place to sit on a summer's evening? Or will it become a focus for imaginative and adventurous play?

Now that people realize that treehouses aren't just for children, a whole industry has grown up to service the requirements of adult clients. These "adult" treehouses may be inspired by any number of needs, from a discreet retreat to a full-on party platform. Although the scale of these concept treehouses may be completely different, the basic construction methods required are pretty similar to a conventional backyard affair. In both cases, there really needs to be a plan drawn up that shows how the treehouse will sit in its tree (or frame) and exactly what

On the grounds of a real castle, a miniature castle grows up in the branches.

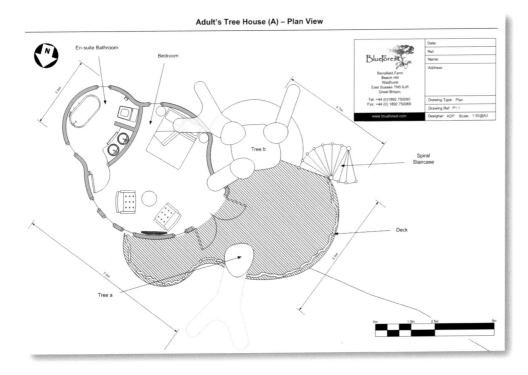

Adult's Tree House (A) – Plan View

En-suite Bathroom

Bedroom

Tree b

Tree a

Spiral Staircase

Deck

BlueForest Design

Bensfield Farm
Beech Hill
Wadhurst
East Sussex TN5 6JR
Great Britain.

Tel: +44 (0)1892 750090
Fax: +44 (0) 1892 750069

www.blueforest.com

Date:	
Ref:	
Name:	
Address:	
Drawing Type:	Plan
Drawing Ref:	P1:1
Designer: ADP	Scale: 1:50@A3

0m   1.5m   2.5m   5m

ABOVE **This computer-generated image shows a highly complex arrangement of treehouses and walkways.**

LEFT **The plan shows how the treehouse will encompass the tree branches.**

These computer-generated renderings show the complex relationship between the treehouse and its tree.

A conventional model can be just as effective as modern technology.

While the floor plans are a great way of working out the internal dimensions of the treehouse and deciding exactly what the space could be used for, these computer visualizations are a wonderful way of showing how the structure will integrate into its setting, take account of any existing elements of the site (like a garden wall), and how the house will sit in its tree. In very mature, multi-branched trees, this can require a fairly complex design solution that is best determined before construction begins. More conventionally, the treehouse architect can also make a three-dimensional model of the proposed construction. This is particularly effective when a multi-building project is envisioned, as it allows the client to have a completely three-dimensional view.

This rendering shows how the treehouse complex will cope with an existing garden wall.

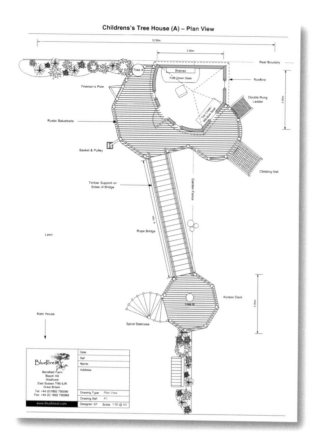

Childrens's Tree House (A) – Plan View

ABOVE **This roofless treehouse drawing shows the internal layout.**

BELOW **This fairytale treehouse is part of an adventure play complex.**

This attractive image shows how the treehouse complex could be built around a small pine grove.

These renderings show several alternative solutions for the same site:

1. A pretty, round treehouse built on a platform around the tree.

2. A less symmetrical treehouse with a thatched roof still built around the tree.

3. Here, the treehouse is supported by an independent frame, while the tree plays host to a large party deck.

4. The tree still supports the party deck and the frame-borne treehouse is larger and less whimsically shaped.

1. The exterior frame of the treehouse.

2. It is now covered in lining paper and batons, ready for the timber cladding.

3. Cedar shingles are fixed to the roof batons.

4. Weatherproof fixings are used.

5. The roof nearing completion.

6. The veranda is completed, while the house awaits its exterior cladding.